DECREES

— FOR —

MEGA

FAVOR

Daily Decrees for Experiencing a Deluge of Favor

MICHELLE J. MILLER

DECREES FOR
MEGA
FAVOR

Daily Decrees for Experiencing A Deluge of Favor

Michelle J. Miller
Author of *Winds of Favor* & *Prophesy to the Wind*

DECREES FOR MEGA FAVOR
By Michelle J. Miller
Published by Michelle J. Miller Ministries International

Printed in the United States of America
Unless otherwise indicated, all scripture taken from the New King James Version® unless. Copyright © 1982 by Thomas Nelson. Used by permission. All rights reserved.

Scripture quotations marked (AMP) are taken from the Amplified Bible, Copyright © 1954, 1958, 1962, 1964, 1965, 1987 by The Lockman Foundation. Used by permission.

Scripture quotations are taken from the New American Standard Bible® (NASB), Copyright © 1960, 1962, 1963, 1968, 1971, 1972, 1973, 1975, 1977, 1995 by The Lockman Foundation Used by permission.
www.Lockman.org

Scripture quotations are from the ESV® Bible (The Holy Bible, English Standard Version®), copyright © 2001 by Crossway, a publishing ministry of Good News Publishers. Used by permission. All rights reserved.

NET Bible® copyright ©1996-2006 by Biblical Studies Press, LLC http://netbible.com All rights reserved.
Holman Christian Standard Bible®
Copyright © 1999, 2000, 2002, 2003, 2009 by Holman Bible Publishers. Used with permission by Holman Bible Publishers, Nashville, Tennessee. All rights reserved.

Visit the author's website at www.michellejmiller.global or www.prophetpreneurs.com or www.brillionairelaw.com

v

CONTENTS

PROPHETIC INTRODUCTION

"And I will make of you a great nation, and I will bless you [with abundant increase of favors] and make your name famous and distinguished, and you will be a blessing [dispensing good to others]."

– Genesis 12:12 (AMPC)

God wants to bless you with abundant increases of favor. God has unlimited favor, and He wants to give you unlimited access to His favor. The favor of God will never run out so you must decree a release of God's favor over your life. The Lord is your shepherd and according to Psalms 23:1, that means you shall not lack. You shall not lack in favor! You can grow in favor with God and with man just like Jesus. As you read this book and make the decrees herein, you will increase in favor.

"And Jesus increased in wisdom and stature, and in favor with God and men." – Luke 2:52 (NKJV)

If Jesus can experience a favor increase, you can experience consistent growth in the area of favor. In fact, the purpose of this book is to not only position you for a favor increase, but for MEGA FAVOR. There are many ways for you to experience MEGA FAVOR, but in this book, we will focus on two methods for experiencing a release of MEGA favor and those methods are (1.) prophecy and (2.) decrees. Prophecy is God's method of using His servants to see and speak His will in the earth. Decrees are the means that Christians operate in their power and authority to speak God's will in the earth. In this book, you are being charged to use these two methods as a means for experiencing mind-blowing MEGA FAVOR in every area of your life.

In this introductory section we will address the issue of prophecy, in Section I we will deal with the topic of decrees, in Section II we will present favor decrees, in Section III we will present a prophetic word entitled *"Heaps of Favor"* that I released on Apostle John Eckhardt's Facebook platform during his 30 days of favor, in Section IV there is bonus content that consists of Favor Confessions released by Apostle John Eckhardt, and finally there is a section for your to C.Y.O.D (Create Your Own Decrees). For the remainder of this section, the content will focus on prophecy and favor. When God wants to do something new, like release MEGA FAVOR, He releases revelation to His servants the prophets and His prophetic people.

"Surely the Lord God does nothing, Unless He reveals His secret to His servants the prophets."
  -    Amos 3:7 NKJV

I want to tell you a kingdom secret, God wants to release MEGA FAVOR over your life. At the time of the writing of this book, the world is entering into the year of 2022. The world has been dealing with a global pandemic for two years, but this pandemic does not stop God's plan to prosper you, bless you, and release His favor upon your life in greater and greater levels. With that being stated, God sent out His servants the prophets from the days of old and He is sending His prophets and prophetic people to release now. In fact, may this book activate and ignite your prophetic call and gift so that God can use you in a greater measure to prophesy as He releases MEGA FAVOR over your life.

"Since the day that your fathers came out of the land of Egypt until this day, I have even sent to you all My servants the prophets, daily rising up

early and sending them." - Jeremiah 7:25 NKJV

If you are a spirit-filled Christian, you have a prophetic flow on the inside of you that just needs to be turned on. If you are currently flowing in the prophetic, God wants you to go deeper into a prophetic lifestyle. I encourage you to simply prophesy an increase of God's favor over the people that as directed by the Holy Spirit:

"For you can all prophesy one by one, that all may learn, and all may be encouraged." - 1 Corinthians 14:31 NKJV

But he who prophesies speaks edification and exhortation and comfort to men. - 1 Corinthians 14:3 NKJV

In fact, I believe as you read this book and make these decrees the Spirit of the Lord will come upon you, and you will prophesy to the point that people see you as a new prophetic person. I believe a prophetic fire and favor will hit your life and your life will be changed.

5

Then the Spirit of the Lord will come upon you, and you will prophesy with them and be turned into another man. - 1 Samuel 10:6 NKJV

Being obedient to God's direction to prophesy favor over the lives of His people changed my life. As I prophesied unique favor experiences over God's people, an increasing jaw-dropping favor begin to flow in my life. As I obeyed God in writing, prophesying, and decreeing favor over the lives of others, I began to experience MEGA FAVOR. You can do this, and you can experience MEGA FAVOR too. In fact, as you read this book, the lion of the tribe of Judah inside you will begin roaring and you will experience a strong unction to prophesy.

A lion has roared! Who will not fear? The Lord God has spoken! Who can but prophesy? - Amos 3:8 NKJV

In the last quarter of 2021, I kept hearing that I need to write another book on favor. I've had this thought in the past, but this time it was very strong. As I pondered and prayed on this, it became clear that I would write a book of favor decrees. While praying and preparing to write, I was reminded of the 30 days of favor that Apostle John Eckhardt hosted on Clubhouse in 2021 and I captured a portion of the release for my personal review. Before writing this book, I was reminded of the day that many of us who joined him on Clubhouse released favor prophecies and decrees. As I listened to mine, my mouth dropped open because during my prophetic release God spoke through me to tell the people it was time for them to begin releasing favor decrees. Immediately below is Apostle John Eckhardt's and my prophetic favor releases from Clubhouse:

"The Lord says that even though it's a new day, it's a new season and many shall confess and decree that I have the favor of God and even when it looks like an unfavorable situation. Even when it looks like your life is not working, and it seems that you're not walking in the path of favor, the Lord says I'm going to cause a light of favor to come upon you in ways that you would have never

known. I'm going to cause you to rise out of that place of feeling as if you're a victim, feeling as if you are at a disadvantage and you're going to rise up. The Lord said, I'm even raising up a generation of overcomers that will overcome the things of the past and the failures of the past and the frustrations of the past. The Lord says I'm calling you into new life by calling you into a new season. I call you into a new place. I call you into a new understanding. I do something new in your life through My Word, and I cause a new fresh grace to come upon you. And not only shall you know about grace, but you shall also have the Spirit of grace.

Not only shall you know about favor, but you shall also see the manifestation of favor in your life in areas that you've not seen it before.

I'm going to cause you to see my miracles of favor, says the Lord.

I'm going to cause you to see even wonders of favor.

I'm going to cause you to be astounded by the immense favor that you'll see in the days to come.

There's coming at dramatic increase in the level of favor that you will walk in.

There's coming even abounding favor, even

multiplied favor is coming upon your life.

And you're going to begin to see miracles and breakthroughs in areas of your life. In areas where it seems as if nothing was happening, you're going to see water come into dry places of your life and water come into the wilderness places. In areas where there seems to have been no productivity, and no prosperity and no abundance, I'm going to break lack off of your life. I'm going to cause poverty to be a thing that no longer will plague you and harass you. I'm going to cause an abundance of relationships. I'm going to even cause you to forget your failure failures in areas of finances and failure areas of relationships. The enemy will not be able to say you're a failure. You're not going to walk in the shame of failure but you're going to even walk in the joy of victory and the joy of success and the joy of prosperity because of My favor. I'm going to cause you even to thank and praise me in ways that you've not done before. I'm going to even take your praise and your worship to another level. You will have a revelation that I am a God of favor. I am a gracious God. I am a kind God. I am a loving God. I am a benevolent God. I am a compassionate God. The Lord says my people have been destroyed for the lack of knowledge, but oh I'm breaking the destruction. No longer will the enemy be able to destroy your life. The devour is being rebuked for your sake, says the Lord. I'm causing you to have victory after victory after victory and the days of sadness and weeping and crying and tears are over and now joy comes. Celebration comes now and you will enjoy life. I come for you to enjoy the abundance of life. I've come to provide for you, says the Lord. So, know even as you renew your mind, study, confess, decree, and believe in the favor that I've given unto you, you'll see favor manifest strongly in the days to come and you'll say oh my God; He was always there. I didn't know it but now I'm seeing the manifestation of it so get ready. For even as the Word of the Lord has come not just 30 days of favor but favor every 30 days.

Every month you'll walk into new favor.

Every month you'll believe me for new breakthroughs.

Every month you'll walk into the new.

Every month you'll walking into even more and more favor.

I release favor upon you. I cause you to walk in favor. I cause you to enjoy favor. I've given favor to you. Favor is my gift to you because I love you. I called you. I've chosen you. I redeemed you. Now, walk in and enjoy this favor and do not feel guilty when favor comes. Don't allow anyone even to cause you to feel as if you don't deserve it. But oh, walk in this favor because of My blood and because of My redemption, you'll see great *breakthroughs, great manifestations, and great favor released in the days to come." – **John Eckhardt**[1]*

After this prophetic word was released, I experienced a favor upgrade. I believe that you experienced a favor upgrade and a favor increase after you read this prophetic release. I believe this prophetic word spoke to the areas of our lives. You might have been experiencing a favor drought before you picked up this book, but you are about to experience a flood of favor. Just as God told Ezekiel to prophesy to the dry bones, and Ezekiel commanded that those dry bones hear the word of the Lord, I believe God told me to write this book as a means for him to water the dry places in your life. This book will release a fresh wind of favor your life.

Again, He said to me, "Prophesy to these bones, and say to them, 'O dry bones, hear the word of the Lord! - Ezekiel 37:4 NKJV

---

[1] Clubhouse, Master the Prophetic Club (April 2021)

On that same day Apostle John released the prophetic word above, I had a Jeremiah experience and God gave me a prophetic word on favor.

Then the Lord put forth His hand and touched my mouth, and the Lord said to me: "Behold, I have put My words in your mouth. - Jeremiah 1:9 NKJV

I believe God supernaturally touched my mouth, put His words in my mouth, and the results was favor increases for the hearers of that prophetic release and now the readers of this book because that prophetic favor release is included here in. Below is that prophetic word:

"These 30 days of favor have been absolutely amazing. I just want to prophesy and decree and declare that your feet are favored. I hear the Lord say I'm about to take your feet into some places where you're going to see new favor as you walk into new rooms and new favor as God opens new doors. I hear God say, go back to some places where it seemed as though you didn't have favor. Go back to places where you were in an unfavorable position because I'm about to switch some things in your favor, says the Lord. I'm about to cause some things that was not decided in your favor to be turned around in your favor, says the Spirit of the Living God.

I hear God say that these are the days that I'm releasing a fresh financial favor over the lives of my sons and my daughters.

These are the days to step out in faith. These are even the days to begin to plow and to trailblaze in the marketplace, says the Spirit of the living God. I am awakening creativity on the inside of you, says the Lord. I'm giving you witty inventions in your dreams. I hear God say, it's time for you to step out in faith. I am going to give you favor with the people that are going to help you. I hear the Lord say don't worry about the money. Don't worry about how it's going to be done. God says My favor is going to make a way for you. God says My favor is going to take you into new streams of income.

I hear God say begin to write out your favor decrees.

Begin to write out what My favor is going to do for you.

Because these are the days of favor manifestation like never before, says the Spirit of the Living God. I hear God say to begin to blow the dust off the visions and dreams that you did not step in because you didn't think you had the favor for it.

I hear God say this is a Kairos time and these 30 days have been the days that I have begun to a dress you, move you, and prepare you to walk into these new doors of favor and in new places favor, says the Spirit of the Living God. I am anointing you to accelerate and an accelerated level of favor is going to come upon you. The things that you

13

thought you were missing in the past; I hear God say I am about to move quickly so things can be done for you fast, so you are not missing anything. I hear God say the things you could not do in the past; My favor is going to get it done for you. I call you up to a new place of favor. I am crowning you with favor.

I hear God say I'm going to even cause you to rule and reign in the marketplace with favor.

I hear God say so take on this favor mantle.

Put on this favor crown.
Take this favor scepter.

Yes, there is a scepter of favor and God says that I'm putting it in your hand and you're going to be able to point it. You're going to make decrees and declarations that will change the lives of people around you, that will change cities, and change nations, and change laws, says the the Spirit of the loving God. So, arise my favored ones because My favor is surrounding you. My favor is all over you and my favor going with you, says God."
– Michelle J. Miller[2]

Because you picked up this book, I want to officially welcome you to your new season of increasing and overflowing favor. People often exclaim that favor isn't fair. However, I disagree

---

[2] Clubhouse, Master the Prophetic Club (April 2021)

with that exclamation because favor is fair. There are numerous scriptures in the bible that address the topic of the favor. God want to give you favor in every area of your life. Not only that, but God also wants to give you MEGA FAVOR. You have found favor with King Jesus, just as Esther found favor with the king.

"Now it came to pass on the third day, that Esther put on her royal apparel, and stood in the inner court of the king's house, over against the king's house: and the king sat upon his royal throne in the royal house, over against the gate of the house. And it was so, when the king saw Esther the queen standing in the court, that she obtained favour in his sight: and the king held out to Esther the golden scepter that was in his hand. So, Esther drew near and touched the top of the scepter. Then said the king unto her, What wilt thou, queen Esther? and what is thy request? it shall be even given thee to the half of the kingdom." – Esther 5:1-3(KJV)

Because you have found favor in the sight of King Jesus, He is holding His scepter out to you and granting your request and as God spoke to me, He is also putting a scepter of favor in your hand so you can release favor over people as you walk in your new season of MEGA FAVOR. It's time for you to receive prophetic words about favor and it's time for you to decree favor.

SECTION I

---◆◇◆---

DECREE A THING

" This decision is by the decree of the watchers, And the sentence by the word of the holy ones, In order that the living may know That the Most High rules in the kingdom of men, Gives it to whomever He will, And sets over it the lowest of men."

– Daniel 4:17 (NKJV)

To experience the manifestation of the promises of God in your life, you need to watch, pray, believe, meditate, declare and decree God's Word over your life. We must decide to agree with the promises of God, watch to see what God is doing in every new season of our life, and then decree what God tells us. The word decree means an official order issued by a legal authority. As an attorney, one document that is very important in my profession is the decree. Judges have legal authority to make ruling decisions in court and they have the power to release decrees in accordance with their judicial decisions. A judge's decree is an official order of business. The Webster's Revised Unabridged Dictionary defines the word "decree" as follows:

"1. (n.) An order from one having authority; deciding what is to be done by a subordinate; also, a determination by one having power; deciding what is to be done or to take place; an edict; authoritative rule or decision.

2. (n.) A decision, order, or sentence, given in a cause by a court of equity or admiralty.

3. (n.) A determination or judgment of an umpire on a case submitted to him.

4. (n.) An edict or law made by a council for regulating any business within their jurisdiction; as, the decrees of ecclesiastical councils.

5. (v. t.) To determine judicially by authority, or by decree; to constitute by edict; to appoint by decree or law; to determine; to order; to ordain; as, a court decrees a restoration of property.

6. (v. t.) To ordain by fate."[3]

7. (v. i.) To make decrees; -- used absolutely.

To make a decree is to have an authoritative order having the force of law. You and I also have been given the power to release decrees.

_____

[3] Webster's Revised Unabridged Dictionary,
https://biblehub.com/topical/d/decree.htm

Our power and authority have been delegated to us by Jesus Christ. In fact, we are responsible for declaring and decreeing God's promises into the earth. When you make decrees, you're making petitions in the Courts of Heaven and God is rendering judgment in your favor. When we release a decree in the earth, we are officially releasing God's Word over our lives concerning the subject of focus. The power of judges making decrees is biblically based and we also see in the bible that kings made decrees. Jesus is the righteous judge, and He is the King of kings who has delegated His authority to rule, reign, judge, declare, and decree to the Saints:

According to **1 Peter 2:9**, we are part of a royal priesthood:

"But you are a chosen people, a royal priesthood, a holy nation, God's special possession, that you may declare the praises of him who called you out of darkness into his wonderful light."

According to **1 Corinthians 6:3**, we will judge angles:

"Do you not know that we shall judge angels? How much more, things that pertain to this life?"

According to **Daniel 7:27**, the dominion and greatness of all of the kingdoms under heaven has been given to the Saints:

"Then the sovereignty, the dominion and the greatness of all the kingdoms under the whole heaven will be given to the people of the saints of the Highest One; His kingdom will be an everlasting kingdom, and all the dominions will serve and obey Him"

According to **Luke 10:19**, the Saints have been given power and authority over all power of the enemy. It's the work of the enemy that tries to stop our decrees from being manifested, but the devil can't stop the plans of God:

"Behold! I have given you authority and power to trample upon serpents and scorpions, and [physical and mental strength and ability] over

all the power that the enemy [possesses]; and nothing shall in any way harm you."

We have been given the power, the authority as well as the kingdom position to make decrees:

And as My Father has appointed a kingdom and conferred it on Me, so do I confer on you [the privilege and decree],
- Luke 22:29 (AMPC)

We have the Word of God, plus the delegated power and authority from Jesus Christ to make decrees. Making decrees is a powerful action step that will literally change our lives. In the bible, Kings made decrees. Below is an example from the Book of Daniel:

I make a decree that in all my royal dominion men must tremble and fear before the God of Daniel, for He is the living God, enduring and steadfast forever, and His kingdom shall not be destroyed, and His dominion shall be even to the end [of the world]. - Daniel 6:26 (APMC)

We are kings and priests according to Revelation 1:6. Because we are positioned as kings and priests, when the early church started the apostles and the elders determined and issues decrees:

And as they went through the cities, they delivered to them the decrees to keep, which were determined by the apostles and elders at Jerusalem. - Acts 16:4 NKJV

You have the power and authority to release decrees that will change your life and the lives of others. Decrees are released from your mouth and life and death is in the power of the tongue (Proverbs 18:21). Decreeing is simply opening your mouth and operating in the power and authority that God has given us within the framework of the Word of God. With that being stated, you have power and authority to decree MEGA FAVOR over every area of your life. You have the power must have kingdom confidence that your decrees will be established in your life:

"You will also declare a thing, And it will be established for you; So, light will shine on your ways." – Job 22:28

As you go to the next section of this book, make these favor decrees with the power and authority. I decree and declare, in accordance with Micah 7:11, that you MEGA FAVOR decree shall go far and wide.

"In the day when your walls are to be built, In that day the decree shall go far and wide." - Micah 7:11 NKJV

SECTION 2

FAVOR DECREES

"You shall also decide and decree a thing, and it shall be established for you; and the light [of God's favor] shall shine upon your ways."

– Job 22:28

Are you ready to experience MEGA FAVOR? MEGA is defined as, *"of the highest level of rank, excellence, or importance; great, large; greatly surpassing others of its kind.*[4]" The bible also gives us a great example of the word MEGA. The great word for great is "megas" (Strong's #3173) and it means *"large, great, in the widest sense."*[5] The KJV translates Strong's #3173 as great 150 times. Accordingly, Strong #3173 is utilized in several scriptures, below are a few examples:

*When Jesus answered and said unto her, O woman, **great is thy faith** be it unto thee even as thou wilt. And her daughter was made whole from that very hour.*
– Matthew 15:28 (KJV)

*But it shall not be so among you: but whosoever will be **great among you**, let him be your minister;*
- Matthew 20:26 (KJV)

*For he shall be **great in the sight of the Lord** and shall drink neither wine nor strong drink; and he shall be filled with the Holy Ghost, even from his mother's womb.*
– Luke 1:5 (KJV)

---

[4] Merriam-Webster Dictionary, https://www.merriam-webster.com/dictionary/mega
[5] BibleHub, https://biblehub.com/greek/3173.htm

*And there came a fear on all: and they glorified God, saying, That a **great prophet** is risen up among us; and, That God hath visited his people. – Luke 7:16 (KJV)*

*And said unto them, Whosoever shall receive this child in my name receiveth me: and whosoever shall receive me receiveth him that sent me: for **he that is least among you all, the same shall be great**
– Luke 9:48(KJV)*

*And with **great power** gave the apostles witness of the resurrection of the Lord Jesus: and great grace was upon them all.
– Acts 4:33(KJV)*

*And Stephen, full of faith and power, did **great wonders and miracles** among the people. – Acts 6:8 (KJV)*

*And being brought on their way by the church, they passed through Phenice and Samaria, declaring the conversion of the Gentiles: and they caused **great joy** unto all the brethren. – Acts 15:33 (KJV)*

*Seeing then that we have a **great high priest**, that is passed into the heavens, Jesus the Son of God, let us hold fast our profession. – Hebrews 4:14(KJV)*

*Now the God of peace, that brought again from the dead our Lord Jesus, that **great shepherd** of the sheep, through the blood of the everlasting*

27

covenant. – Hebrews 13:20
*I was in the Spirit on the Lord's day, and heard behind me a **great voice**, as of a trumpet. – Revelation 1:10(KJV)*

*And the seventh angel sounded; and there were **great voices** in heaven, saying, The kingdoms of this world are become the kingdoms of our Lord, and of his Christ; and he shall reign for ever and ever.*
– Revelations 11:15(KJV)

*Saying, We give thee thanks, O Lord God Almighty, which art, and wast, and art to come; because thou hast taken to thee thy **great power**, and hast reigned.*
– Revelations 11:17 (KJV)

Megas (Strong's #3173) is also translated to mean the following:

- Abundant;
- All the more;
- Greater;
- Greater things;
- High;
- Big;
- Huge;
- Large;
- Fierce;

- Mighty;
- Strong;
- Long time and so much more.

God wants to give us a great amount of favor. God wants us to have favor in abundance. Because we have power and authority through Jesus Christ, we can decree MEGA FAVOR over our lives. Jesus experienced growth in wisdom, and favor and so can we. The following biblical translations of Jesus growth in favor provide a great picture of what mega favor looks like:

*And Jesus **grew** in wisdom and stature, and in favor with God and man.*
– Luke 2:52

*And Jesus **increased** in wisdom and in stature and in favor with God and man.*
– Luke 2:52 (ESV)

*And Jesus **continued to advance** in wisdom and stature, and in favor with God and men. –*
Luke 2:52 (BLB)

*And Jesus **kept increasing** in wisdom and in stature, and in favor with God and men.*

29

Jesus is a great example of favor expansion. The favor on the life of Jesus experienced growth. The favor on our life can also experience growth. We can grow in favor, we can advance in favor, and the favor on our lives can keep increasing until we experience MEGA FAVOR. The bible mentions another person who grew in favor and that person is Samuel.

"And the child Samuel grew in and in favor both with the LORD and men." – 1 Samuel 2:26

God has an unlimited supply of favor available just for you. As you make the favor decrees in this book, do not doubt that God is more than able to release a strong wind of favor over your life.

If you are ready to experience MEGA FAVOR in your life, it's time for you to open your mouth and decree it. I love the instructions in Job 22:28 because before the instruction to make a decree, there is the instruction to decide. You must decide to agree with God's Word about favor. You must decide to believe that God not only wants to release favor over your life, but He wants to release MEGA FAVOR over your life. After you have decided that God's unlimited favor is you for you, it's time to decree it over your life. You must decide and decree. When we decree the Word of God, we are releasing the decree in faith and confidence. Decrees cause the truths of the heavenly realm to manifest into the physical realm. God has favor stored up for us in heaven so when we release decrees, the truth of God promises to bless us and favor us is released into our lives. When we make decrees God's heavenly treasury is unlocked to resource the decrees. Let's make the favor decrees in this section every day.

TIME & FAVOR

There's an opportune time to do things, a right time for everything on the earth: A right time for birth and another for death, A right time to

*plant and another to reap, A right time to kill
and another to heal, A right time to destroy and
another to construct, A right time to cry and
another to laugh, A right time to lament and
another to cheer, A right time to make love and
another to abstain, A right time to embrace and
another to part, A right time to search and
another to count your losses, A right time to
hold on and another to let go, A right time to rip
out and another to mend, A right time to shut
up and another to speak up, A right time to love
and another to hate, A right time to wage war
and another to make peace.
– Ecclesiastes 3:1-8*

*You will arise and have mercy on Zion; For the
time to favor her, Yes, the set time, has come. –
Psalms 102:13*

*Look carefully then how you walk, not as
unwise but as wise, making the best use of the
time, because the days are evil. – Ephesians
5:15-16*

*For he says, "In the time of my favor I heard
you, and in the day of salvation I helped you." I
tell you, now is the time of God's favor, now is
the day of salvation.
– 2 Corinthians 6:2*

*For his anger is but for a moment, and his favor
is for a lifetime. Weeping may tarry for the
night, but joy comes with the morning.
– Psalms 30:5*

Thus says the Lord: "In a time of favor I have answered you; in a day of salvation, I have helped you; I will keep you and give you as a covenant to the people, to establish the land, to apportion the desolate heritages." – Isaiah 49:8

Ask your young men and they will tell you. Therefore, let my young men find favor in your sight, for we come at an opportune time. I pray you, give whatever you have at hand to your servants and to your son David.
– 1 Samuel 25:8

I decree and declare that it is my set time of MEGA FAVOR.

I decree and declare that every time someone see me, they will give me MEGA FAVOR.

I decree and declare that every time I wake up in the morning, I wake up with MEGA FAVOR.

I decree and declare that NOW is the time of God's MEGA FAVOR.

I decree and declare that it's time for MEGA

It is the set time for God to release MEGA FAVOR over my life.

It is the set time for God to release f MEGA FAVOR over my household.

It is the set time for God to release MEGA FAVOR over my family.

It is the set time for God to release MEGA FAVOR over my ministry.

It is the set time for God to release MEGA FAVOR over my job.

It is the set time for God to release MEGA FAVOR over my business.

It is the set time for God to release MEGA FAVOR over my household.

I decree and declare that this is my hour of MEGA FAVOR.

I decree and declare that every day is a day of MEGA FAVOR for me.

I decree and declare that I am entering into a new era of MEGA FAVOR.

This is my season of MEGA FAVOR.

This is my year of MEGA FAVOR.

It is my time and my turn for MEGA FAVOR.

I decree and declare that I have MEGA FAVOR for a lifetime.

I decree and declare that I will be a good steward over my set time of MEGA FAVOR.

It's my Chronos time of MEGA FAVOR.

It is my Kairos time of MEGA FAVOR.

It is my appointed time of MEGA FAVOR.

It is opportune moment of f MEGA FAVOR.

It is my due season of MEGA FAVOR.

I decree and declare that I will use my time, finances, influence, and position to sow MEGA FAVOR into others' lives.

I decree and declare that I will have a lifetime of joy and great satisfaction in God's MEGA FAVOR.

I decree and declare that I will have a lifetime of MEGA FAVOR.

WISDOM & FAVOR

So, Pharaoh said to Joseph, "You're the man for us. God has given you the inside story—no one is as qualified as you in experience and wisdom. From now on, you're in charge of my affairs; all my people will report to you. Only as king will I be over you." – Genesis 41:39-40 (MSG)

God gave Solomon wisdom—the deepest of understanding and the largest of hearts. There was nothing beyond him, nothing he couldn't

*handle. Solomon's wisdom outclassed the
vaunted wisdom of wise men of the East,
outshone the famous wisdom of Egypt. He was
wiser than anyone—wiser than Ethan the
Ezrahite, wiser than Heman, wiser than Calcol
and Darda the sons of Mahol. He became
famous among all the surrounding nations. He
created 3,000 proverbs; his songs added up to
1,005. He knew all about plants, from the huge
cedar that grows in Lebanon to the tiny hyssop
that grows in the cracks of a wall. He
understood everything about animals and
birds, reptiles, and fish. Sent by kings from all
over the earth who had heard of his reputation,
people came from far and near to listen to the
wisdom of Solomon. – 1 Kings 4:29-34 (MSG)*

*King Solomon was wiser and richer than all the
kings of the earth—he surpassed them all.
People came from all over the world to be with
Solomon and drink in the wisdom God had
given him. And everyone who came brought
gifts—artifacts of gold and silver, fashionable
robes, and gowns, the latest in weapons, exotic
spices, and horses and mules—parades of
visitors, year after year. – 1 Kings 10:23-25
(MSG)*

*For whoever finds me [Wisdom] finds life and
draws forth and obtains favor from the Lord. –
Proverbs 8:35*

*For the Lord gives wisdom; from his mouth
come knowledge and understanding;*

- Proverbs 2:6

Good understanding gains favor, But the way
of the unfaithful is hard.
– Proverbs 13:15

A good person's mouth is a clear fountain of
wisdom; a foul mouth is a stagnant swamp. –
Proverbs 10:31 (MSG)

The king's favour [is] toward a wise servant:
but his wrath is [against] him that causeth
shame. – Proverbs 14:35(AMPC)

Wisdom is better when it's paired with money,
Especially if you get both while you're still
living. Double protection: wisdom and wealth!
Plus, this bonus: Wisdom energizes its owner. –
Ecclesiastes 7:11-12 (AMPC)
The words of a wise man's mouth are gracious
and win him favor, but the lips of a fool
consume him. – Ecclesiastes 10:12

The queen heard of the hysteria among the
king and his nobles and came to the banquet
hall. She said, "Long live the king! Don't be
upset. Don't sit around looking like ghosts.
There is a man in your kingdom who is full of
the divine Holy Spirit. During your father's time
he was well known for his intellectual brilliance
and spiritual wisdom. He was so good that
your father, King Nebuchadnezzar, made him
the head of all the magicians, enchanters,
fortunetellers, and diviners. There was no one
quite like him. He could do anything—interpret

*dreams, solve mysteries, explain puzzles. His
name is Daniel, but he was renamed
Belteshazzar by the king. Have Daniel called
in. He'll tell you what is going on here." –
Daniel 510-12 (MSG)*

*And rescued him out of all his afflictions and
gave him favor and wisdom before Pharaoh,
king of Egypt, who made him ruler over Egypt
and over all his household. – Acts 7:10*

*And the child grew and became strong, filled
with wisdom. And the favor of God was upon
him. – Luke 2:40
And Jesus increased in wisdom and in stature
and in favor with God and man.
– Luke 2:52*

I decree and declare that God gives me MEGA
WISDOM & MEGA FAVOR.

I decree and declare that I have MEGA
UNDERSTANDING & MEGA FAVOR.

I decree and declare that I have a MEGA
MINDSET.

Because my words are wise, I win MEGA
FAVOR.

I decree and declare that God rescues me out
of all of my afflictions, and He gives me MEGA
FAVOR & MEGA WISDOM.

MEGA WISDOM is better with MEGA WEALTH, so I have them both.

I decree and declare that God gives me the inside stories and I have a MEGA WISDOM ADVANTAGE.

I decree and declare that the King of king's favor is towards me because I am His wise servant.

I decree and declare that I find wisdom and obtain favor.

I decree and declare that I have wisdom, understanding, and favor.

I decree and declare that God helps me to be skillful in wisdom and well-favored.

I decree and declare that I have double protection: wisdom & wealth.

My mouth is a fountain of wisdom.

I am smart.

I am clever.

I am intelligent.

I am wise.

I am brilliant.

I am perceptive.

I have good judgment.

I am discerning.

Wisdom energizes me.

I decree and declare that I will grow in wisdom and favor all the days of my life.

I decree and declare that I daily increase in wisdom and in favor.

HUMILITY & FAVOR

And Joshua son of Nun was full of the spirit of wisdom, for Moses had laid his hands upon him; so, the Israelites listened to him and did as the Lord commanded Moses. – Deuteronomy 34: (AMPC)

Solomon's wisdom excelled the wisdom of all the people of the East and all the wisdom of Egypt. – 1 Kings 4:30 (AMPC)

And all the earth sought the presence of Solomon to hear his wisdom which God had put in his mind.
– 1 Kings 10:24 (AMPC)

Toward the scorners he is scornful, but to the humble he gives favor. – Proverbs 3:34

Pride lands you flat on your face; humility prepares you for honors. – Proverbs 29:23 (MSG)

But he gives us more grace. That is why Scripture says: "God opposes the proud but shows favor to the humble." – James 4:6

In the same way, you who are younger, submit yourselves to your elders. All of you, clothe yourselves with humility toward one another, because "God opposes the proud but shows favor to the humble."
– 1 Peter 5:5

Therefore, humble yourselves under the mighty hand of God, that He may exalt you at the proper time, - 1 Peter 5:6

o the king said to Ziba, "Here, all that belongs to Mephibosheth is yours." And Ziba said, "I humbly bow before you, that I may find favor in your sight, my lord, O king!" – 2 Samuel 16:4

As I humbly bow down to worship God, He gives me MEGA FAVOR.

Because I walk in MEGA HUMILITY, I have MEGA FAVOR.

My MEGA HUMILITY prepares me for MEGA HONORS and MEGA FAVOR.

God shows MEGA FAVOR to the MEGA HUMBLE.

People will seek my presence to hear my MEGA WISDOM and God will give me MEGA FAVOR with these people.

I humble myself under the mighty hand of God and He gives me MEGA FAVOR.

I decree and declare that I clothed myself in humility.

God opposes the proud, but because I am humble, He favors me.

The wisdom God gives me excels the wisdom of people of the world.

I am not wise in my own eyes; I obtain wisdom from God.

I decree and declare that I am obedient, and I am favored.

I decree and declare that I am submissive, and I am favored.

I decree and declare that I am meek, and I am favored.

I decree and declare that I am modest, and I am favored.

I decree and declare that I am compassionate, and I am favored

I decree and declare that I am witty, and I am favored.

I decree and declare that I am blessed, and I am favored.

I decree and declare that I am clothed in MEGA WISDOM and MEGA FAVOR.

I decree and declare that humility has prepared me for MEGA FAVOR.

PROTECTION & FAVOR

Then God was right before him, saying, "I am God, the God of Abraham your father and the God of Isaac. I'm giving the ground on which you are sleeping to you and to your descendants. Your descendants will be as the dust of the Earth; they'll stretch from west to east and from north to south. All the families of the Earth will bless themselves in you and your descendants. Yes. I'll stay with you, I'll protect you wherever you go, and I'll bring you back to this very ground. I'll stick with you until I've done everything, I promised you."
– Genesis 28:13-15 (MSG)

Then God was right before him, saying, "I

43

*am God, the God of Abraham your father and
the God of Isaac. I'm giving the ground on
which you are sleeping to you and to your
descendants. Your descendants will be as the
dust of the Earth; they'll stretch from west to
east and from north to south. All the families of
the Earth will bless themselves in you and your
descendants. Yes. I'll stay with you,*
*I'll protect you wherever you go, and I'll bring
you back to this very ground. I'll stick with you
until I've done everything, I promised you."*
*Thou hast granted me life and favour, and thy
visitation hath preserved my spirit. – Job 10:12*

*Glory to God in the highest heaven, and on
earth peace to those on whom his favor rests. –
Luke 2:14*

*For you bless the righteous, O Lord; you cover
him with favor as with a shield. – Psalm 5:12*

*God's angel sets up a circle of protection
around us while we pray.
– Psalm 34:7 (MSG)*

*My enemies cannot triumph over me because
the Lord has favored me. - Psalm 41:11*

*For the Lord God is a Sun and Shield; the Lord
bestows [present] grace and favor and [future]
glory (honor, splendor, and heavenly bliss)! No
good thing will He withhold from those who
walk uprightly.
– Psalm 84:11(AMPC)*

44

But God, dear Lord, I only have eyes for you.
Since I've run for dear life to you, take good
care of me. Protect me from their evil scheming,
from all their demonic subterfuge. Let the
wicked fall flat on their faces, while I walk off
without a scratch.
– Psalm 141:8-10 (MSG)

God's name is a place of protection— good
people can run there and be safe.
- Proverbs 18:10 (MSG)

Lord, You will ordain peace (God's favor and
blessings, both temporal and spiritual) for us,
for You have also wrought in us and for us all
our works. – Isaiah 26:12(AMPC)

God provides MEGA PROTECTION and MEGA
FAVOR for me.

God gives me MEGA PEACE and His MEGA
FAVOR RESTS ON ME.

God grants me MEGA LIFE and MEGA
FAVOR.

God covers me with a MEGA SHIELD OF
FAVOR.

My enemies can't triumph over me because I
have MEGA FAVOR.

I am God's favorite one and He preserves my spirit.

God's name is a place of protection for me.

As I pray, there's a circle of angelic protection around me.

The Lord is my Sun and Shield, and He bestows grace, favor, and glory upon me.

The Lord watches over me.

The Lord is my covering.

The Lord is my fortress.

The Lord is my guard.

The Lord is my defense.

The Lord is my shelter.

The Lord is my safeguard.

The Lord is my security.

The Lord is a wall of protection around me.

The Lord protects me from every scheme, plot, and plan of the enemy.

The Lord watches over me.

The provides MEGA FAVOR and MEGA PROTECTION to me and my family.

REVERSALS & FAVOR

And said, If it please the king, and if I have found favour in his sight, and the thing [seem] right before the king, and I [be] pleasing in his eyes, let it be written to reverse the letters devised by Haman the son of Hammedatha the Agagite, which he wrote to destroy the Jews which [are] in all the king's provinces: - Esther 8:5(AMPC)

If someone steals an ox or a lamb and slaughters or sells it, the thief must pay five cattle in place of the ox and four sheep in place of the lamb. If the thief is caught while breaking in and is hit hard and dies, there is no bloodguilt. But if it happens after daybreak, there is bloodguilt. "A thief must make full restitution for what is stolen. The thief who is unable to pay is to be sold for his thieving. If caught red-handed with the stolen goods, and the ox or donkey or lamb is still alive, the thief pays double. – Exodus 22:1-4 (MSG)

If someone grazes livestock in a field or vineyard but lets them loose so they graze in someone else's field, restitution must be made from the best of the owner's field or vineyard. – Exodus 22:5 (MSG)

47

Behold, I have received a command to bless;
He has blessed, and I cannot reverse it.
– Numbers 23:20

So, David inquired of the Lord, saying, "Shall I
pursue this troop? Shall I overtake them?" And
He answered him, "Pursue, for you shall surely
overtake them and without fail recover all." – 1
Samuel 30:8

So, sing, Daughter Zion! Raise your voices,
Israel! Daughter Jerusalem, be happy!
celebrate! God has reversed his judgments
against you and sent your enemies off chasing
their tails. From now on, God is Israel's king, in
charge at the center. There's nothing to fear
from evil ever again! – Zephaniah 3:14-15
(MSG)

Because of God's MEGA FAVOR on my life, I
experience MEGA REVERSALS.

I decree and declare that every negative letter
or document written about me will undergo a
MEGA REVERSAL.

Every thief that has stolen from me must
make MEGA RESTITUTION.

Because of the MEGA FAVOR on my life, if
people misuse me those people must provide
MEGA REPAYMENTS from the best of what
they own.

I decree and declare that every letter, document, decree, form, or policy written to destroy me shall be reversed.

I decree and declare that every certification, license, petition, or contract working against my life will be annulled and rendered void.

I decree and declare that laws and policies that are ungodly and unjustly impact my life will be repealed.

I decree and declare that every false statement, slanderous statement, and libel will be retracted.

I decree and declare that any and all contracts or agreements that have terms that are not in my favor shall be canceled.

I decree and declare that God reverses every judgment written against me.

I decree and declare that I will pursue what belongs to me, overtake my enemies and without fail recover everything that belongs to me.

I decree and declare that every person that decided an issue against me shall rescind that decision.

I decree and declare that every policy that has terms that work against my favor shall be voided.

I decree and declare that every person who decided against me shall have a change in heart and reverse the decision.

I decree and declare that I experience MEGA FAVOR for DIVINE REVERSALS.

WEALTH & FAVOR

Barzillai the Gileadite had come down from Rogelim. He crossed the Jordan with the king to give him a good send-off. Barzillai was a very old man—eighty years old! He had supplied the king's needs all the while he was in Mahanaim since he was very wealthy. – 2 Samuel 19:31-32 (AMPC)
God answered Solomon, "This is what has come out of your heart: You didn't grasp for money, wealth, fame, and the doom of your enemies; you didn't even ask for a long life. You asked for wisdom and knowledge so you could govern well my people over whom I've made you king. Because of this, you get what you asked for—wisdom and knowledge. And I'm presenting you the rest as a bonus— money, wealth, and fame beyond anything the kings before or after you had or will have." – 2 Chronicles 1:11-12 (MSG)

Wealth and riches will be in his house, And his righteousness endures forever. – Psalm 112:3

A good name is to be more desired than great wealth, Favor is better than silver and gold. – Proverbs 22:1

So, you will find favor and good success in the sight of God and man. – Proverbs 3:4

Sloth makes you poor; diligence brings wealth. – Proverbs 10:4 (MSG)

Who could ever find a wife like this one— she is a woman of strength and mighty valor! She's full of wealth and wisdom. The price paid for her was greater than many jewels. – Proverbs 31:10 (TPT)

And when the king saw Queen Esther standing in the court, she won favor in his sight, and he held out to Esther the golden scepter that was in his hand. Then Esther approached and touched the tip of the scepter. – Esther 5:2

Let the favor of the Lord our God be upon us and establish the work of our hands upon us; yes, establish the work of our hands! – Psalm 90:17
You may say to yourself, "My power and the strength of my hands have produced this wealth for me." But remember the LORD your God, for it is he who gives you the ability to produce wealth, and so confirms his covenant, which he swore to your ancestors, as it is today. – Deuteronomy 8:17-18

*Let them shout for joy and be glad, Who favor
my righteous cause; And let them say
continually, "Let the Lord be magnified, Who
has pleasure in the prosperity of His servant." –
Psalm 35:27*

*Unending wealth and glory come to those who
discover where I dwell. The riches of
righteousness and a long, satisfying life will be
given to them. – Proverbs 6:19 (TPT)*

*I will give you the treasures of darkness And
hidden riches of secret places, That you may
know that I, the Lord, Who call you by your
name, Am the God of Israel.
– Isaiah 45:3*

*Blessed (happy, to be envied, and spiritually
prosperous—with life-joy and satisfaction in
God's favor and salvation, regardless of their
outward conditions) are the poor in spirit (the
humble, who rate themselves insignificant), for
theirs is the kingdom of heaven! – Matthew
5:3(AMPC)*

*The best you can do with your life is have a
good time and get by the best you can. The
way I see it, that's it—divine fate. Whether we
feast or fast, it's up to God. God may give
wisdom and knowledge and joy to
his favorites, but sinners are assigned a life of
hard labor, and end up turning their wages
over to God's favorites. Nothing but smoke—
and spitting into the wind. – Ecclesiastes 2:24-
26 (MSG)*

I have MEGA WEALTH and MEGA FAVOR.

Mature wealthy people will provide MEGA SUPPLIES to take care of my needs.

I have MEGA FAVOR with people who have MEGA WEALTH.

The MEGA FAVOR of God is upon me, and He establishes the work of my hands.

I have MEGA FAVOR and MEGA SUCCESS with God and with man.

My diligence brings me MEGA WEALTH.

God is presenting MEGA MONEY, MEGA WEALTH, AND MEGA FAME as a bonus for me seeking His wisdom and knowledge.

MEGA WEALTH and MEGA RICHES are in my household.

I win favor with kings, influencers, leaders, and officials.

I win favor in court cases, administrative cases, legal reviews, and mediations.

God gives me favor and the power to produce wealth.

I favor God's righteous causes and He takes pleasure in my prosperity.

I decree and declare that I am naturally prosperous and wealthy.

I decree and declare that I am spiritually prosperous and wealthy.

The wages of sinners are turned over to me.

I decree and declare that God grants me MEGA FAVOR and gives me the treasures of darkness

I decree and declare that God grants me MEGA FAVOR and gives me hidden riches in secret places.

I decree and declare that I am full of MEGA FAVOR, wealth, and wisdom.

Because I walk in the MEGA FAVOR of God, I have unlimited resources.

I decree and declare that I receive continuous increases of capital.

I decree and declare that I receive continuous increases of cashflow.

My real estate assets increase and make me wealthy.

My business assets increase and make me wealthy.

My intellectual property assets increase and make me wealthy.

My digital assets increase and make me wealthy.

I decree and declare that I build wealth on the earth.

I decree and declare that I build wealth on social media platforms.

I decree and declare that I build wealth in the metaverse.

I decree and declare that I build wealth in virtual reality platforms.

I decree and declare that I build wealth in alternative reality platforms.

I decree and declare that I build wealth through foreign currency.

I decree and declare that I build wealth through cryptocurrency.

I decree and declare that I build wealth with stocks.

I decree and declare that I build wealth with dividends.

I decree and declare that I build wealth with contracts.

I decree and declare that I build wealth with partnerships.

I decree and declare that I build wealth with join ventures.

I decree and declare that I build wealth with mergers & acquisitions.

I decree and declare that I build wealth with securities.

I decree and declare that I build wealth with commodities.

I decree and declare that I build wealth with oil and mineral rights.

I decree and declare that I build wealth with silver and gold.

I decree and declare that I build wealth with diamonds and precious jewels.

I decree and declare that I receive wealth and MEGA FAVOR in abundance.

I decree and declare that I have multiple streams of income.

I decree and declare that I have more than enough.

I decree and declare that I am superabundant.

I decree and declare that I receive and earn thousands.

I decree and declare that I receive and earn thousands of thousands.

I decree and declare that I receive and earn millions.

I decree and declare that I receive and earn millions of millions.

I decree and declare that I receive billions.

I decree and declare that I have MEGA FAVOR and MEGA RICHES and MEGA WEALTH is in my house.

BLESSINGS & FAVOR

And he blessed him and said, Blessed (favored with blessings, made blissful, joyful) be Abram by God Most High, Possessor and Maker of heaven and earth, - Genesis 14:9(AMPC)

Dwell temporarily in this land, and I will be with you and will favor you with blessings; for to you and to your descendants I will give all these lands, and I will perform the oath which I swore to Abraham your father. – Genesis 26:3

Then Isaac sowed seed in that land and received in the same year a hundred times as much as he had planted, and the Lord favored him with blessings.
– Genesis 26:12

And the Lord appeared to him the same night and said, I am the God of Abraham your father. Fear not, for I am with you and will favor you with blessings and multiply your descendants for the sake of My servant Abraham. – Genesis 26:24

That you will do us no harm, inasmuch as we have not touched you and have done to you nothing but good and have sent you away in peace. You are now the blessed or favored of the Lord! – Genesis 26:29

Let peoples serve you and nations bow down to you; be master over your brothers and let your mother's sons bow down to you. Let everyone be cursed who curses you and favored with blessings who blesses you. – Genesis 27:9

For you had little before I came, and it has increased and multiplied abundantly; and the Lord has favored you with blessings wherever I turned. But now, when shall I provide for my own house also? – Genesis 30:30(AMPC)

And of Naphtali he said, O Naphtali, satisfied with favour, and full with the blessing of the LORD: possess thou the west and the south. – Deuteronomy 33:23

58

And the Lord appeared to him the same night and said, I am the God of Abraham your father. Fear not, for I am with you and will favor you with blessings and multiply your descendants for the sake of My servant Abraham. – Genesis 26:24

And of Asher he said: "Asher is most blessed of sons; Let him be favored by his brothers, And let him dip his foot in oil. – Deuteronomy 33:24

Rich blessings overflow with every encounter with you, and you placed a royal crown of gold upon his head. – Psalm 21:3 (TPT)

Blessing after blessing comes to those who love and trust the Lord. They will not fall away, for they refuse to listen to the lies of the proud. – Psalm 40:40 (TPT)

Great blessing and wealth fill the house of the wise, for their integrity endures forever. – Psalm 1123 (TPT)

God can pour on the blessings in astonishing ways so that you're ready for anything and everything, more than just ready to do what needs to be done. As one psalmist puts it, He throws caution to the winds, giving to the needy in reckless abandon. His right-living, right-giving ways never run out, never wear out. This most generous God who gives seed to the farmer that becomes bread for your meals is more than extravagant with you. He gives you something you can then give away, which

grows into full-formed lives, robust in God,
wealthy in every way, so that you can be
generous in every way, producing with us great
praise to God.
– 2 Corinthians 9:8-11 (MSG)

I decree and declare that I am now the MEGA
BLESSED and MEGA FAVORED of the Lord.

I decree and declare that I receive MEGA
BLESSINGS and MEGA FAVOR.

I decree and declare that I am favored with
MEGA BLESSINGS.

I decree and declare that I sow MEGA SEEDS
and receive a one-hundred-fold return.

Everyone that favors me with blessings
receives blessings.

I decree and declare that God favors me with
blessings wherever I turn.

I decree and declare that I am satisfied with
favor and full of blessings.

I decree and declare that God is with me, and
He will favor me with blessings.

I decree and declare that I am the most
blessed.

Rich blessings and favor flow into the lives of
everyone that encounter me.

I am favored so blessings after blessings comes continuously into my life.

I decree and declare that I am wise, so great and wealth fill my life.

I decree and declare that God pours out blessings into my life in astonishing ways.

I have blessings and the grace of God are upon my life.

The MEGA FAVOR God on my life brings me great benefits.

The MEGA FAVOR of God on my life causes people to show me kindness.

The MEGA FAVOR of God on my life causes people to give me gifts.

The MEGA FAVOR of God on my life causes people to come to my aid.

The MEGA FAVOR of God on my life gives me an advantage in every area of life.

The MEGA FAVOR of God on my life grants me approvals.

The MEGA FAVOR of God grants me blessings and goodwill in every area of my life.

LIGHT & FAVOR

Now when the turn of Esther, the daughter of Abihail the uncle of Mordecai, who had taken her for his daughter, was come to go in unto the king, she required nothing but what Hegai the king's chamberlain, the keeper of the women, appointed. And Esther obtained favour in the sight of all of them that looked upon her. – Esther 2:15

The Lord make His face to shine upon and enlighten you and be gracious (kind, merciful, and giving favor) to you; - Numbers 6:25(AMPC)

And I will give this people favor in the sight of the Egyptians; and when you go, you shall not go empty.
- Exodus 3:21

You shall also decide and decree a thing, and it shall be established for you; and the light [of God's favor] shall shine upon your ways. – Job 22:28(AMPC)

"This is the way God works. Over and over again He pulls our souls back from certain destruction, so we'll see the light—and live in the light! – Job 33:29-30 (MSG)

Restore us again, O God of hosts; and cause Your face to shine [upon us with favor as of old], and we shall be saved! – Psalm 80:7

"And now," God says, this God who took me in hand from the moment of birth to be his servant, To bring Jacob back home to him, to set a reunion for Israel— What an honor for me in God's eyes! That God should be my strength! He says, "But that's not a big enough job for my servant— just to recover the tribes of Jacob, merely to round up the strays of Israel. I'm setting you up as a light for the nations so that my salvation becomes global!" – Isaiah 49:5-6 (MSG)

"The kind of fasting I want is this: Remove the chains of oppression and the yoke of injustice and let the oppressed go free. Share your food with the hungry and open your homes to the homeless poor. Give clothes to those who have nothing to wear, and do not refuse to help your own relatives. "Then my favor will shine on you like the morning sun, and your wounds will be quickly healed. I will always be with you to save you; my presence will protect you on every side. When you pray, I will answer you. When you call to me, I will respond. – Isaiah 58:6-9 (GNT)

"'Men and women who have lived wisely and well will shine brilliantly, like the cloudless, star-strewn night skies. And those who put others on the right path to life will glow like stars forever. – Daniel 12:3 (MSG)

Jesus once again addressed them: "I am the world's Light. No one who follows me stumbles around in the darkness. I provide plenty of light to live in." – John 8:12 (MSG)

But Paul and Barnabas didn't back down. Standing their ground they said, "It was required that God's Word be spoken first of all to you, the Jews. But seeing that you want no part of it—you've made it quite clear that you have no taste or inclination for eternal life—the door is open to all the outsiders. And we're on our way through it, following orders, doing what God commanded when he said, I've set you up as light to all nations. You'll proclaim salvation to the four winds and seven seas!" – Acts 13:40-41 (MSG)

Remember, our Message is not about ourselves; we're proclaiming Jesus Christ, the Master. All we are messengers, errand runners from Jesus for you. It started when God said, "Light up the darkness!" and our lives filled up with light as we saw and understood God in the face of Christ, all bright and beautiful. – 2 Corinthians 4:5-6 (MSG)

There is a MEGA LIGHT OF FAVOR on my life.
My face is shining with MEGA FAVOR.
God gives me MEGA FAVOR in the sight of everyone that meets me.

I live in a MEGA LIGHT of MEGA FAVOR.

The LIGHT OF GOD'S MEGA FAVOR shine upon my ways.

GOD is setting me up as a MEGA LIGHT to the nations.

When I leave interactions with people, I will not leave empty-handed because the light of God's MEGA FAVOR on my life.

I decree and declare that God's face shine upon me with MEGA FAVOR.

When I fast, the MEGA FAVOR of God shines upon me.

I decree and declare that Because I live wisely and well in God's sight, I shine brilliantly.

Like Jesus, I am the world's light.

God favors me and He had set me up as a light to all nations.

I decree and declare that I light up the darkness.

I decree and declare that I have a glow of MEGA FAVOR.

I decree and declare that I illuminate with MEGA FAVOR.

I decree and declare that I radiate MEGA FAVOR.

I decree and declare that I shine with MEGA FAVOR.

I decree and declare that I have a MEGA FAVOR sparkle on my life.

I decree and declare that I am beaming with MEGA FAVOR.

I decree and declare that have a MEGA FAVOR flare.

I decree and declare that I have a MEGA FAVOR afterglow.

I decree and declare that there is a MEGA FAVOR brilliance upon my life.

INCREASE & FAVOR

And I will make of you a great nation, and I will bless you [with abundant increase of favors] and make your name famous and distinguished, and you will be a blessing [dispensing good to others].
– Genesis 12:2 (AMPC)

Jacob replied, "You know well what my work has meant to you and how your livestock has flourished under my care. The little you had

66

when I arrived has increased greatly;
everything I did resulted in blessings for you.
Isn't it about time that I do something for my
own family?" – Genesis 30:29-30 (MSG)

Thus, the man increased and became
exceedingly rich, and had many sheep and
goats, and maidservants, menservants,
camels, and donkeys. – Genesis 30:43

But the descendants of Israel were fruitful
and increased abundantly; they multiplied and
grew exceedingly strong, and the land was full
of them. – Exodus 1:7

'For I will look on you favorably and make you
fruitful, multiply you and confirm My covenant
with you. – Leviticus 26:9

You open Your hand and satisfy every living
thing with favor. – Psalm 45:16

Increase my greatness (my honor) and turn and
comfort me. – Psalm 71:21

There [the Lord] greatly increased His people
and made them stronger than their oppressors.
– Psalm 105:24 (AMPC)

May the Lord give you increase more and more,
you and your children.
– Psalm 115:114

To proclaim the accepted and acceptable year of the Lord [the day when salvation and the free favors of God profusely abound]. – Luke 4:19 (AMPC)

They make a lot of sense, these wise folks; whenever they speak, their reputation increases.
– Proverbs 16:23 (MSG)

"And this is what will happen: You will increase and prosper in the land. The time will come"—God's Decree! — "when no one will say any longer, 'Oh, for the good old days! Remember the Ark of the Covenant?' It won't even occur to anyone to say it— 'the good old days.' The so-called good old days of the Ark are gone for good. – Jeremiah 3:1-16 (MSG)

For out of His fullness (abundance) we have all received [all had a share, and we were all supplied with] one grace after another and spiritual blessing upon spiritual blessing and even favor upon favor and gift [heaped] upon gift.
– John 1:16 (AMPC)

May grace (God's favor) and peace (which is perfect well-being, all necessary good, all spiritual prosperity, and freedom from fears and agitating passions and moral conflicts) be multiplied to you in [the full, personal, precise, and correct] knowledge of God and of Jesus our Lord. – 2 Peter 1:2 (AMPC)

MEGA FAVOR INCREASES over my life, all the days of my life.

God blesses me with MEGA FAVOR and ABUNDANT INCREASES OF FAVORS.

The little that I have will experience MEGA INCREASE.

The little that other people have will experience MEGA INCREASE when I come into their lives.

The MEGA FAVOR of God INCREASES GREATLY over my life.

I have MEGA FAVOR and I INCREASE ABUNDANTLY.

I decree and declare that God increases me, and I will become exceedingly rich.

I decree and declare that I increase in MEGA FAVOR and fruitfulness.

I decree and declare that God will look upon me favorably and make He makes me fruitful.

I decree and declare that God increases the f MEGA FAVOR and MEGA HONOR upon my life daily.

I decree and declare that God satisfies me with MEGA FAVOR.

The MEGA FAVOR of God increases upon my life and my reputation increases.

I decree and declare that whenever I speak, my reputation increases.

I decree and declare that God gives me and my children continuous increases from generation to generation.

I decree and declare that I will increase and prosper in the land that God sends me to.

I decree and declare that God favors me and blessings upon blessings are being released over my life.

I decree and declare that I daily experience increases in natural blessings.

I decree and declare that I daily experience increases in spiritual blessings.

I decree and declare that I receive MEGA FAVOR upon MEGA FAVOR.

I decree and declare that I experience increases in MEGA FAVOR all the days of my life.

I decree and declare that God multiplies the MEGA FAVOR on my life.

I decree and declare that God expands the expands the level of MEGA FAVOR on my life.

I decree and declare that the MEGA FAVOR of God on my life is being amplified daily.

I decree and declare that MEGA FAVOR is increasing and building up over my life.

The MEGA FAVOR of God is flooding into my life, and I experience a favor overflow daily.

I decree and declare that I experience a deluge of MEGA FAVOR.

I decree and declare that I experience an influx of MEGA FAVOR.

I decree and declare that I experience a MEGA FAVOR boost today.

I decree and declare that I am being inundated with MEGA FAVOR.

I decree and declare that the MEGA FAVOR of God gushes into every area of my life.

I decree and declare that I have an oversupply of MEGA FAVOR.

I decree and declare that I have plenty of MEGA FAVOR.

I decree and declare that I am being submerged in MEGA FAVOR.

I decree and declare that MEGA FAVOR runs over into my life, and I never run out of MEGA FAVOR.

I decree and declare that I am soaked in MEGA FAVOR.

I decree and declare that God drenches me in MEGA FAVOR.

I decree and declare that I have MEGA FAVOR r in superabundance.

PROMOTION & FAVOR

For you are the glory of their strength; by your favor our horn is exalted. – Psalm 89:17

Prize Wisdom highly and exalt her, and she will exalt and promote you; she will bring you to honor when you embrace her.
– Proverbs 4:8(AMPC)

When good people are promoted, everything is great, but when the bad are in charge, watch out! – Proverbs 28:12 (MSG)

So, Joseph found favor in his sight and attended him, and he made him overseer of his house and put him in charge of all that he had.
– Genesis 39:4

*He who speaks in a [strange] tongue
edifies and improves himself, but he who
prophesies [interpreting the divine will and
purpose and teaching with inspiration]
edifies and improves the church and promotes
growth [in Christian wisdom, piety, holiness,
and happiness]. – 1 Corinthians 14:4 (AMPC)*

*So be content with who you are, and don't put
on airs. God's strong hand is on you;
he'll promote you at the right time. Live carefree
before God; he is most careful with you. – 1
Peter 5:6-7 (MSG)*

*And after you have suffered a little while, the
God of all grace [Who imparts all blessing and
favor], Who has called you to His [own] eternal
glory in Christ Jesus, will Himself complete and
make you what you ought to be, establish and
ground you securely, and strengthen, and
settle you.
– 1 Peter 5:10*

I receive continuous MEGA PROMOTION
because of the MEGA FAVOR on my life.

God favors me and my horn experience MEGA
EXALTATION.

The MEGA FAVOR and MEGA WISDOM exalts
me and positions me for MEGA PROMOTIONS.

I will find MEGA FAVOR in this sight of kings,
leaders, influences, executives, government
officials, diplomats, and dignitaries and I will

be promoted to management and leadership positions.

God's strong hand of favor is upon me, and he promotes me.

God will promote me at the right time.

I decree and declare that the MEGA FAVOR of God promotes me.

I decree and declare that the MEGA FAVOR of God advances me.

I decree and declare that the MEGA FAVOR of God grants me breakthroughs.

I decree and declare that the MEGA FAVOR of God gives me a boost in ministry and in the marketplace.

I decree and declare that the MEGA FAVOR of God gives me upgrades.

I decree and declare that the MEGA FAVOR of God elevates me.

I decree and declare that the MEGA FAVOR of God exalts me.

I decree and declare that the MEGA FAVOR of God helps me further my vision and my goals.

I decree and declare that the MEGA FAVOR of God causes me to step up.

I decree and declare that the MEGA FAVOR of God cases me to move up.

I decree and declare that the MEGA FAVOR of God causes me to rise up in life.

I decree and declare that the MEGA FAVOR of God causes me to have sponsors.

I decree and declare that the MEGA FAVOR of God causes me to progress in every area of my life.

I decree and declare that the MEGA FAVOR of God raises me up from a low place to a high place.

THE BEST & FAVOR

"Now, my son, listen to me. Do what I tell you. Go to the flock and get me two young goats. Pick the best; I'll prepare them into a hearty meal, the kind that your father loves. Then you'll take it to your father, he'll eat and bless you before he dies." Genesis 27:8-10 (MSG)

So, Pharaoh commissioned Joseph: "I'm putting you in charge of the entire country of Egypt." Then Pharaoh removed his signet ring from his finger and slipped it on Joseph's hand. He outfitted him in robes of the best linen and put a gold chain around his neck. He put the second-in-command chariot at his disposal,

*and as he rode people shouted "Bravo!" Joseph
was in charge of the entire country of Egypt. –
Genesis 41:41-43 (MSG)*

*Pharaoh said to Joseph, "Tell your brothers,
'This is the plan: Load up your pack animals;
go to Canaan, get your father and your
families, and bring them back here. I'll settle
you on the best land in Egypt—you'll live off
the fat of the land.' – Genesis 45:17-18 (MSG)*

*"Also tell them this: 'Here's what I want you to
do: Take wagons from Egypt to carry your little
ones and your wives and load up your father
and come back. Don't worry about having to
leave things behind; the best in all of Egypt will
be yours.'" - Genesis 45:17-18 (MSG)*

*Now the young woman pleased him, and she
obtained his favor; so, he readily gave beauty
preparations to her, besides her allowance.
Then seven choice maidservants were provided
for her from the king's palace, and he moved
her and her maidservants to the best place in
the house of the women. – Esther 2:9
The king loved Esther more than all the other
women, and she obtained grace and favor in
his sight more than all the virgins; so, he set
the royal crown upon her head and made her
queen instead of Vashti. – Esther 2:17*

*Now we have not received the spirit [that
belongs to] the world, but the [Holy] Spirit Who
is from God, [given to us] that we might realize
and comprehend and appreciate the gifts [of*

divine favor and blessing so freely and lavishly] bestowed on us by God. – 1 Corinthians 2:12

For all [these] things are [taking place] for your sake, so that the more grace (divine favor and spiritual blessing) extends to more and more people and multiplies through the many, the more thanksgiving may increase [and redound] to the glory of God. – 2 Corinthians 4:15 (AMPC)

And God is able to make all grace (every favor and earthly blessing) come to you in abundance, so that you may always and under all circumstances and whatever the need be self-sufficient [possessing enough to require no aid or support and furnished in abundance for every good work and charitable donation]. – 2 Corinthians 9:8 (AMPC)

"You also get the Wave-Offerings from the People of Israel. I present them to you and your sons and daughters as a gift. This is the standing rule. Anyone in your household who is ritually clean may eat it. I also give you all the best olive oil, the best new wine, and the grain that is offered to God as the firstfruits of their harvest—all the firstfruits they offer to God are yours. Anyone in your household who is ritually clean may eat it. – Numbers 18:11-13 (MSG)

No expense was spared—everything here, inside, and out, from foundation to roof was constructed using high-quality stone,

*accurately cut and shaped and polished. The
foundation stones were huge, ranging in size
from twelve to fifteen feet, and of the
very best quality. The finest stone was used
above the foundation, shaped to size, and
trimmed with cedar. The courtyard was
enclosed with a wall made of three layers of
stone and topped with cedar timbers, just like
the one in the porch of The Temple of God. – 1
Kings 7:9-12*

*Forget that I sowed wild oats; Mark me with
your sign of love. Plan only the best for
me, God! -Psalm 25:7 (MSG)*

I receive MEGA FAVOR for THE BEST.

Because of the MEGA FAVOR on my life
people will select the BEST ITEMS for me.

Because of the MEGA FAVOR on my life
people will select the BEST CLOTHING for me.

Because of the MEGA FAVOR on my life
people will select the BEST LAND for me.

Because of the MEGA FAVOR on my life, if I
lost anything in my past, I will recover it.

God will grant me the BEST OF PRODUCTS
and the BEST LAND.

Because of the MEGA FAVOR on my life, I
receive extra.

Because of the MEGA FAVOR on my life, I will be offered the BEST PLACES to stay.

I decree and declare that God gives me a crown of MEGA FAVOR.

I decree and declare that I receive the best of oils.

I decree and declare that I receive the best of clothing.

I decree and declare that I receive the best of lands.

I decree and declare that I receive the best of opportunities,

I decree and declare that the best doors are opened up to me.

I decree and declare that I will speak in the best platforms.

I decree and declare that I will connect with the best people.

I decree and declare that I receive high-quality items.

I decree and declare that I receive the finest of products.

I decree and declare that I walk in MEGA FAVOR, and I experience the choicest options.

I decree and declare that I walk in MEGA FAVOR, and I experience outstanding opportunities.

I decree and declare that I walk in MEGA FAVOR, and I experience first-rate options.

I decree and declare that I walk in MEGA FAVOR, and I have incomparable experiences.

I decree and declare that I walk in MEGA FAVOR, and I have a-list people as contacts, customers, and clients.

I decree and declare that I walk in MEGA FAVOR, and I have elite experiences.

I decree and declare that I walk in MEGA FAVOR, and I am placed in the most advantageous positions.

I decree and declare that I walk in MEGA FAVOR, and I am suddenly placed in first-class seats.

I decree and declare that I walk in MEGA FAVOR, and I have premium products and services.

MEGA FAVOR

For six months he put on exhibit the huge wealth of his empire and its stunningly beautiful royal splendors. At the conclusion of the exhibit, the king threw a weeklong party for everyone living in Susa, the capital—important and unimportant alike. The party was in the garden courtyard of the king's summer house. The courtyard was elaborately decorated with white and blue cotton curtains tied with linen and purple cords to silver rings on marble columns. Silver and gold couches were arranged on a mosaic pavement of porphyry, marble, mother-of-pearl, and colored stones. Drinks were served in gold chalices, each chalice one-of-a-kind. The royal wine flowed freely—a generous king! – Esther 1:4-7 (AMPC)

And with great strength and ability and power the apostles delivered their testimony to the resurrection of the Lord Jesus, and great grace (loving-kindness and favor and goodwill) rested richly upon them all. – Acts 4:33(AMPC)

And the grace (unmerited favor and blessing) of our Lord [actually] flowed out superabundantly and beyond measure for me, accompanied by faith and love that are [to be realized] in Christ Jesus.
- 1 Timothy 1:14(AMPC)

"Listen. What do you make of this? A farmer planted seed. As he scattered the seed, some of it fell on the road and birds ate it. Some fell in the gravel; it sprouted quickly but didn't put down roots, so when the sun came up it withered just as quickly. Some fell in the weeds; as it came up, it was strangled among the weeds, and nothing came of it. Some fell on good earth and came up with a flourish, producing a harvest exceeding his wildest dreams.
– Mark 4:3-8 (MSG)

I decree and declare that I am MARKED FOR MEGA FAVOR.

I decree and declare that I am a MEGA FAVOR MAGNET.

I decree and declare that the light of God's MEGA FAVOR is upon my life.

I decree and declare that I experience a MEGA FAVOR surge every day.

I decree and declare that I experience a downpour of MEGA FAVOR every day.

I decree and declare that I wake up with MEGA FAVOR.

I decree and declare that I go to sleep with MEGA FAVOR.

I decree and declare that throughout my day, I experience MEGA FAVOR with God and with man.

I decree and declare that God has unlimited MEGA FAVOR stored up just for me.

I decree and declare that I speak as a person with MEGA FAVOR.

I decree and declare that I have a shield of MEGA FAVOR.

I decree and declare that MEGA FAVOR surrounds me.

I decree and declare that I walk in MEGA FAVOR.

I decree and declare that I live in MEGA FAVOR.

I decree and declare that I wake-up with MEGA FAVOR.

I decree and declare that my ministry has MEGA FAVOR.

I decree and declare that my non-profit organization has MEGA FAVOR.

I decree and declare that my business has MEGA FAVOR.

I decree and declare that I have a MEGA FAVOR testimony.

I decree and declare that I am a MEGA FAVOR success story.

I decree and declare that everywhere I go I experience MEGA FAVOR.

I decree and declare that everyone who sees me gives me MEGA FAVOR.

I decree and declare that I release MEGA FAVOR.

I decree and declare that I am a MEGA FAVOR catalyst.

I decree and declare that double doors of MEGA FAVOR are opening for me.

I decree and declare that my children have MEGA FAVOR.

I decree and declare that my children's children have MEGA FAVOR.

I decree and declare that there is an unstoppable MEGA FAVOR being released upon my life.

I decree and declare that MEGA GRACE and MEGA FAVOR rest richly upon me.

I decree and declare that unmerited MEGA FAVOR flow superabundantly and beyond measure for me.

I decree and declare that I have unlimited MEGA FAVOR.

I decree and declare that the MEGA FAVOR flowing in my life is immeasurable.

I decree and declare that the MEGA FAVOR on my life is endless and unrestricted.

I decree and declare that there is MEGA FAVOR on my bank accounts.

I decree and declare that there is MEGA FAVOR on my business accounts.

I decree and declare that there is MEGA FAVOR on my investment accounts.

I decree and declare that there is MEGA FAVOR on my retirement accounts.

I decree and declare that there is MEGA FAVOR on my life to accumulate personal property.

I decree and declare that there is MEGA FAVOR on my life to accumulate commercial property.

I decree and declare that there is MEGA FAVOR on my life to accumulate rental property.

I decree and declare that there is MEGA FAVOR on my life to accumulate investment property.

I decree and declare that there is MEGA FAVOR on my life to buy boats.

I decree and declare that there is MEGA FAVOR on my life to buy yachts.

I decree and declare that there is MEGA FAVOR on my life to buy islands.

I decree and declare that there is MEGA FAVOR on my trusts.

I decree and declare that I have never-ending MEGA FAVOR.

I decree and declare that God gives me a deluge of MEGA FAVOR.

I decree and declare that I have HEAPS MEGA FAVOR without end.

I decree and declare that MEGA FAVOR is piling up in every area of my life.

I decree and declare that I have MEGA FAVOR financial favor.

I decree and declare that I have MEGA RIDICULOUS FAVOR.

I decree and declare that The WINDS OF MEGA FAVOR are blowing over my life.

I decree and declare that I have MEGA FAVOR without end.

I decree and declare that I experience MEGA FAVOR everywhere.

SECTION 3

HEAPS OF FAVOR

" When Hezekiah and the princes came and saw the heaps, they blessed the Lord and His people Israel. 9 Then Hezekiah questioned the priests and Levites about the heaps. 10 Azariah the high priest, of the house of Zadok, answered him, Since the people began to bring the offerings into the Lord's house, we have eaten and have plenty left, for the Lord has blessed His people, and what is left is this great store." – 2 Chronicles 31:8-10

Good wants to give us MEGA FAVOR and MEGA BLESSINGS on an unlimited basis. God wants favor to heap up in your life. The word "heaps" is not used often in the bible, especially not in a positive sense, so the scriptures that address the topic of blessings and heaps stand out.

Rich blessings overflow with every encounter with you, and you placed a royal crown of gold upon his head.4 He wanted life[b]—you have given it to him and more! The days of his blessing stretch on one after another, forever!5 You have honored him and made him famous. Glory-garments are upon him, and you surround him with splendor and majesty. 6 Your victory heaps blessing after blessing upon him. What joy and bliss he tastes, rejoicing before your face! – Psalm 21:3-6 (TPT)

God himself will fill you with more. Blessings upon blessings will be heaped upon you and upon your children from the maker of heaven and earth, the very God who made you! – Psalm 115:14-15 (TPT)

God gave me a message I entitled "Heaps of Favor" that I shared on social media. Initially, that message was going to be included in my book, "Winds of Favor," but I sensed that it wasn't time to share that message in a book. To heap up means to *collect in great quantity; load heavily; and bestow lavishly or in large quantities.*[6] When I began writing this book, I sensed that the "Heaps of Favor" message belongs in this book. The section is an edited and redacted version of that HEAPS OF FAVOR message:

"The other day I was sitting at my desk and papers were piling up. For some reason, I was just focusing on those piles. As I focused on those piles of paper, the word "heaps" came to me. Then I heard the Lord say, I'm about to release heaps of favor; the favor that I am releasing over My people is going to have heaps of favor. What does that mean? That means the favor that God is releasing upon

---

[6] Merriam-Webster Dictionary, https://www.merriam-webster.com/dictionary/heap

you is not going to be one level of favor. It's not going to be one dimension of favor.

God is about to release heaps of favor.

What does "heaps of favor" mean? That means favor is about to pile up on your behalf. That means favor is not about to stop but you're about to see a growth of favor.

When I prophesy heaps of favor are being released, this means favor will pile up and pile up and pile up. God has been releasing ridiculous favor. God has been releasing extreme favor; He has been releasing an explosion of favor. I've heard favor testimonies of how God favor is being released upon the people of God. Because of favor, God says He's expanding your influence. God is causing you to have the things that you need because the favor is coming to you in abundance. But again, we have to make sure that our response is proper.

We must glorify God as we get greater and greater levels of favor.

We have to make sure that we don't get puffed up; we must remain in a place of humility, and we must remain teachable. God can begin to bestow upon you more and more favor. Apostle John Eckhardt has shared that there are things you can do to position yourself to receive favor.

One of the things you can do to position yourself for favor from God is to be a giver.

Givers receive favor. You cannot buy favor just like you cannot buy blessings. You can't buy titles. You can't buy certain things. But one thing you can do is humble yourself and make a sacrifice. You're giving is a sacrifice even on today when we go into our respective churches. You give God a sacrifice of praise, right? One of the things that God will cause us to do when we give Him a sacrifice of praise to also give seeds sacrificially.

Sometimes God will have us to give where it hurts, to give when it seems like we don't have the ability to give. However, you know when there is sowing the law of God also reaping. When you sow, your harvest is piling up in heaps. If you sow favor, there's also a season of reaping. Your seed sowing begins to heap up and when your sewing begins to heap up for reaping begins to heap up. God is saying if you want me to release heaps of favor you need to sow heaps of favor.

Do you know you can begin sowing in heaps today? You can sacrifice your time; you give your tithes and you're offering. As you sow your time, your financial resources, and favor you will position yourself for prosperity and favor will bring abundance to you. You will heap up so much favor that you will have favorable market distinction upon your life.

As you receive heaps of favor, God will begin to set you apart and the favor of God will give you special blessings and opportunities.

The favor of God will open special doors for you. I want to share this scripture with you. This scripture is not something I looked at in the context of favor in the past. In this

94

scripture there's an example, some people decided to give and give until the point where there was more than enough. There's basic favor, then there's abundant favor and there's a flow of favor. Gods is saying you don't have to lose favor. The level of favor on your life can continue to go to higher and higher and higher and higher and higher. Favor can begin to expand. Favor can grow. The Lord showed me an example and that example if with laundry. If you have been preparing to wash clothes, but kept putting it off, this laundry begins to pile up. When you don't do your laundry, you end up with a heap of clothes. God said look, just like you see clothing pile up and heap up, He said, just imagine favor beginning to pile up and he upon your life. Let me the scripture.

2 Chronicles 31

I am in 2 Chronicles and I'm going to share what it looks like when people give in heaps. I'm going to start at verse five so we can see this in the context of a natural king issuing a decree, but we also know that the is the King of kings. When the King of kings releases a command and when he released a decree when he says now is the set time of favor and is time for me to release favor food on my sons and my daughters, everything under the sun has to come into alignment with the commandment.

Nothing, no one, and no devil in hell can stop what God has commanded.

When God commands His blessings and command His favor to come upon you, no one can withdraw it. Nobody can take it away. All people can do is see the blessings and favor come on your life, but they can't take it. The enemy can come and begin to form weapons, but those weapons cannot prosper. Anything that God will have done for you shall and will be done. When God commands something to happen, it's not a might, and it is not a maybe, but it is something that God will be faithful to. Why because God is faithful to His word to perform it and God is faithful to what

He says. Ok, now let's go to our scripture: 2 Chronicles 31 starting at verse five.

> *'As soon as the order went out, the Israelites generously gave the firstfruits of their grain, new wine, olive oil and honey and all that the fields produced. They brought a great amount, a tithe of everything. 6 The people of Israel and Judah who lived in the towns of Judah also brought a tithe of their herds and flocks and a tithe of the holy things dedicated to the Lord their God, and they piled them in heaps. 7 They began doing this in the third month and finished in the seventh month. 8 When Hezekiah and his officials came and saw the heaps, they praised the Lord and blessed his people, Israel. 9 Hezekiah asked the priests and Levites about the heaps; 10 and Azariah the chief priest, from the family of Zadok, answered, "Since the people began to bring their contributions to the temple of the Lord, we have had enough to eat and plenty to spare, because the Lord has blessed his people, and this great amount is left over.'*

- 2 Chronicles 31:5-10

Glory to God. God wants His people to have great abundance. God is ready to release heaps of favor upon your life. As you sacrifice your time for Him and as you give your plans and purposes of God, God will bless you. As you sow into the lives of men and women of God, God is going to command His blessings and favor to fall upon your life. The Lord began to show me a prophetic picture of heaps. The Lord says, My command has gone out and because My command has gone out to those of the authority, those in power, the kings of this earth, they're coming to you with heaps.

People of influence are coming to give you heaps so you can have more than enough.

You're going to a place in life where heaps of blessings and favor will fall upon your life. People around you will start asking you what's going on in your life. People want to know what's happening because they see heaps of blessings and favor piling up in your life. This is exactly what happened in the scripture (2 Chronicles 31:9). Hezekiah the king asked the Levites about the heaps. The response was people just keep giving. God wants to take you into a dimension and this new dimension of giving will begin to unlock some things into your life. Your giving will cause you to go into a place of abundance; a place when you will start receiving the heaps. God wants you to enter into a cycle of favor. The favor God is releasing is going to continue to take you into new places and God and new dimensions of God's glory.

God says get ready for the heaps.

Get ready for heaps of blessing. Get ready to give in heaps, but also get ready to receive in heaps.

Get ready to sow in heaps and get ready to reap in heaps, says the Lord.

Get ready for my favor to pile up in your life, says the Lord.

I'm going to take you from glory to glory and strength to strength, says the Lord.

I'm about to take you to new levels of favor, says the Lord.

Favor is coming in your life in heaps.

Favor is going to continue to grow and grow and grow over your life.

I hear the Lord say hold on.... I'm activating something that will change the trajectory of your life...

God says it is the set time to favor Zion. Yes, we are Zion. We are that holy place we are those holy people of God and when the set time of favor has come like this, there's a cycle of abundance that comes upon your life. There's a cycle that comes on upon your life where you begin to prosper. When you look in 2 Chronicles 31:10, the people began to say we have plenty. In this scripture is a picture of what you can have. You can have enough to eat, enough to handle your business, enough to take care of your basic needs, enough for tithes & offering, and still have plenty left.

You're going to have plenty left over.

Don't you want to go into the place where the Lord God begins to position you so that you have plenty left over?

Do you want to be in a position where you have plenty left over? We serve a God that will make sure you have plenty left over. Some people don't like leftovers. However, give me some favor that's leftover. God want us to have so much favor that not only are we a conduit of His favor, but we will also begin releasing favor and we still have plenty favor left over.

You can have favor in abundance

You can have heaps of favor.

SECTION 4

BONUS CONFESSIONS

Favor Confessions by Apostle John Eckhardt

The following favor confessions was released by Apostle John Eckhardt after he did a FB live broadcast entitled "30 Days of Favor.[7]" People share these Favor Confessions on numerous websites and many social media outlets. You should make these favor confessions along with the decrees in this book:

---

[7] Favor Confessions by John Eckhardt,
https://www.facebook.com/294531486518/posts/10156447733761519/

I have Favor with God and man

I have an Abundance of Favor

I wear the crown of Favor

I walk in the Path of Favor

I wear the Coat of Favor

I drink from the Fountain of Favor

I harvest from the Field of Favor

I live by the River of Favor

I am covered by the Flood of Favor

I am overwhelmed by an Avalanche of Favor

My cup runs over with Favor

I draw from the Well of Favor

I am impacted by the Winds of Favor

I am revived by the Breath of Favor

104

I am soaked in the Rain of Favor

I live under the Cloud of Favor

I am refreshed by the Dew of Favor

I am a Recipient of the King's Favor

I walk in Extraordinary Favor

I live with Unusual Favor

I obtain Ridiculous Favor

I enjoy Extreme Favor

I have a Lifetime of Favor

I reap Heaps of Favor

I will never Lack Favor

I always Increase in Favor

I have an Anointing for Favor

I have Gifts that Bring Favor

My Relationships are Favored

I am Rich with Favor

I have strong Faith for Favor

I am Surrounded by Favor

Favor locates me.

Favor follows me.

Favor is my portion in life.

I enjoy Financial Favor

I have Favor in my city

I have Mega Favor

Favor flows out of my life like a river

I sow Favor

I enjoy new Favor

I receive the Word of Favor

I will sing about Favor

I praise the LORD for Favor

I come to the throne of Favor

I walk in the revelation of Favor

I understand Favor

Wisdom gives me Favor

I associate with those who are Favored

I am Highly Favored

Favor is multiplied in my life.

SECTION 6

CREAT YOUR OWN CONFESSIONS

Confessions by _____

_____

_____

_____

_____

_____

_____

_____

_____

_____

ABOUT THE AUTHOR

Michelle is a strong apostolic-prophetic voice called to the nations, and she is the Founder of Michelle J. Miller Ministries International. Michelle is an international intellectual property, business & entertainment attorney. Michelle is also an international speaker, best-selling author, and business coach. She is the Founder & Chief Esquire Officer of The M. J. MILLER Law Firm®, the Creator of The Law Box®, and Prophetpreneur Global University's Founder. ™ In addition to her bachelor's and Law degrees, Michelle has an advanced law degree (LLM) in International Business & Trade Law and a Doctor of Ministry in Theology.

Michelle has traveled the words for ministry, business, and law. Her most recent ministry book. *Prophesy to the Wind* is a #1 Amazon New Release and Best Seller. Michelle has the heart to help people understanding that the Kingdom of God is here, and Christians are called to rule and reign on the earth as Ambassadors of Jesus Christ. Michelle has a passion for teaching, training, equipping, and activating people in prophetic ministry. Michelle believes there is a clarion call for more prophets and prophetic people to take their place as God's bold, courageous, and influential prophetic voices in the marketplace. Michelle is a prophetic pusher that ignites people to step into their Kingdom purpose in ministry and the marketplace.

The M. J. MILLER Law Firm® is a boutique law firm focused on Trademarks & Copyrights, Business, Contacts, and Media/Entertainment. We provide confidential and excellent services to ensure that our clients make well-informed decisions to ensure clients receive maximum results from our business relationship. Michelle had over fifteen years of legal experience, primarily serving as a senior-level attorney in a corporate legal department before opening the firm. Michelle has extensive experience advising clients on cutting-edge legal issues on a local, national, and international level. Michelle has created and negotiated multi-million-dollar contracts and provided primary legal support for business operations globally. Michelle's latest book, *"REGISTERED: A Guide for Protecting Your Brand, Business and Bucks with Trademarks,"* is a #1 Amazon New Release and #9 Best Seller. Michelle's newest endeavor, the Prophetpreneur Global University™, is an online, faith-based business and prophetic marketplace ministry university that help people excel in their industries while making money in ways that honor God. Overall, Michelle J. Miller and The M. J. MILLER Law Firm® is the undeniable law office of choice for business and brand protection and expansion.

Michelle has submitted every area of her life to the Lord. She resides in the Chicagoland, IL area with her daughter. She is committed to championing the works that God has set before and continuously representing King Jesus in everything that she does.

Website:

www.michellejmiller.global

WINDS
of
FAVOR

MICHELLE J. MILLER

PROPHESY
TO THE
Wind

**Prophecies & Declarations
for Navigating the Winds of God**

MICHELLE J. MILLER.
Author of Winds of Favor

21 Days of
Fasting for
Favor

Michelle J. Miller
Author of Winds of Favor

LORD
TEACH ME TO
PROFIT

30 Biblical Principles for Experiencing
Marketplace Prosperity & Favor

MICHELLE J. MILLER

FOREWORD BY JOHN ECKHARDT

THIS GENERATION

END TIME PROPHETIC TEACHING OF JESUS

MICHELLE J. MILLER

Foreword by LaJun M. Cole, Sr.

POSSESS THE KINGDOM

It's Time To Rule & Reign, Not Rapture

MICHELLE J. MILLER
Author of This Generation

www.ingramcontent.com/pod-product-compliance
Lightning Source LLC
Chambersburg PA
CBHW051430090426
42737CB00014B/2895

9 781734 686234